Poems From The Heartland

A Collection of Poetry

By Tom Paulding

Published by Happy Jack Publishing, LLC

Copyright © 2014 Tom Paulding

All rights reserved.

ISBN:1495335143
ISBN-13:9781495335143

DEDICATION

To Mary Frances

CONTENTS

ACKNOWLEDGMENTS

I want to thank my sidekick of 50 years, Mary Frances, and my daughter, Ramona. This publication was made possible by Beth Burgmeyer, who used her literary/publishing skills to make these works available for everyone to enjoy.

PART ONE
REFLECTIONS FROM THE HEART

THE DEVIL IS MY DATE

A summer night in '58
And I'd just turned sixteen
My dad he bought a brand new car
Like none I'd never seen

A brand new Pontiac Star Chief
It was the real deal
A piece of steel sent from above
The fastest thing on wheels

That's so many years ago
Now a Lincoln is my ride
And tonight no girl does ride with me
For the Devil's by my side

I would do one hundred thirty
Going down the Cotter flats
And the troopers that did see me
Said "My God man what was that!"

Now all that's left are memories
Even Jesus I can't find
I say old friend I'm right down here
But I think he must be blind

So one last run upon that flat
And at last I know my fate
For I found the one that understands
You see the Devil is my date

1986

I watch the snow through tear filled eyes
Covering fields far below
With memories of another time
Where there my crops did grow

Another time, a joyous time
When this land it was my life
And in those times I did not know
Of trouble or of strife

But then my world came to an end
With my lender as my foe
Now I am driven from my land
But have nowhere to go

Now every hope and every dream
Does die with the auction cry
But in my heart and in my soul
God knows how I did try

Bringing pennies on the dollar
And still I'm in the red
I shake my head and slowly bow
Wishing, Lord, that I were dead

Now as I watch those fields of white
Which below lies loam and sand
I wipe a tear and walk away
For the bank now owns my land

My eyes they search the heavens
Searching past the sky of grey
And with His love to guide me
I'll win another day

A PATRIOT

I guess you would call me a liberal
And I've always felt proud and free
Now I'm talking to the right wing
And the troubles that I see

They talk about the Tea Party
And the southern redneck states
And social justice that we've earned
I would like a true debate

I truly am so grateful
That I've stood for what is right
Because you right wing diplomats
Are on this land a fearsome blight

Now I think of King and Kennedy
And of the progress we have made
But now a bunch of brain dead fools
Want to take it all away

In 2012 our time has come
We will not hesitate
For the real patriots of this land
Will step up to the plate

THE AUCTIONEER

He climbs the block and takes his seat
Tips his hat then says hello
With mike in hand he turns the switch
And his words begin to flow

We'll start the sale with heifers boys
They're choice so let's begin
Forty thousand pounds, a thousand each
He says with a tiny grin

The buyers stand around the rail
With no smiles upon their face
Then the auctioneer he starts the day
And begins his rhythmic pace

His dimes turn into dollars
Then his gavel does come down
Sold sixty dollars and a quarter
Now the farmers start to frown

The dust it boils inside the barn
And the drafts sell oh so fast
He says my friends I'll swear to God
These low prices cannot last

CHICAGO MERCANTILE

I met him in Chicago
On Maxwell Street I think
He said, "Could you spare a quarter?
For I really need a drink"

His outstretched hand was trembling
But I caught a twinkle in his eye
I handed him a quarter
Then asked him the reason why

We sat down on a park bench
The two of us that day
He said, "I've got quite a story
So listen to what I say"

With a trembling voice he told me
That once he had made the grade
How he was the best floor trader
On the Chicago Board of Trade

He said, "I then hit the Merc and Bellies
To be rich I took a pledge
Then one day I risked it all
And put on a Texas Hedge"

He said, "My boy, that fateful day
The victor was the Bear
Now all I have is a memory
And this suit that I still wear"

"I lost my wife and family
And my money on that day
It was seven million dollars
That I pissed away"

"Now, son, I've got to leave you
To buy a jug of wine
And do you believe that when I drink that stuff
For a while things are fine"

He said, "Goodbye" and walked away
My soul felt a fiery sting
For the Chicago Merc is where I work
In the Bellies I know I'm King.

THE GREATEST OF THEM ALL

I've been an auctioneer my friend
For thirty years or so
I've heard some chants lighting fast
And others oh so slow

Then I met a man named Hilpipre
He had risen into fame
He said don't call me Mister
For Merv it is my name

I talked with him for quite some time
And could have learned much more
But I asked him what he loved the most
"When I became world champ in two thousand four"

He's still a cryin' auctions
With the greatest of them all
Dressed in a suit and Stetson hat
None other walks so tall

THE REAL COWBOY

There are a lot of cowboys
With rhinestone boots and hats
With brand new trucks and trailers
Now what the hell is that

They ride their horse around the ring
And never give a thought
That most the judges lack cowboy sense
And a lot of them's been bought

But I met a true old cowboy
Just the other day
He had just got done a shoeing a horse
And was off to bale some hay

His hat was kinda dirty
And he drove a beat up truck
His eyes they showed a lot of years
When he had been down some on his luck

He would spin to me a line or two
Some happy and some blue
But when I got to know him
I found most of them were true

He's one of the real American cowboys
Who still walks upon this land
And if you ever meet him
You will truly understand

FORTY-ONE MEN

The year was 1864
And this young lad headed west
Across the plains and mountains high
I knew I was the best

Forty-one men did try me
Forty they would die
And when their final breath was drawn
Not a tear fell from my eye

At night I slept in cheap hotels
Or brothels filled with whores
And every time I paid them
They just walked out of the door

Forty one slingers did try me
And forty they did fail
Before I drew my dying breath
I had to tell my tale

Forty men had a weakness
For they had someone so near
For me I had not a single soul
So for death I had no fear

But then a lad got jealous
For me a sleepin' with his whore
And fired a bullet through my chest
This time he walked out the door

Now you know my story
Every word of it is true
And up in this bed I'm dying
Just a lad of twenty-two

SLEEP

I went to sleep a thinkin'
What a great meal my wife prepared
Then I heard on the latest evening news
Two million kids had not so fared

I couldn't sleep as I lay my head
With my wife there next to me
For we had lived the American dream
So blind we could not see

I do not have the answers
But I'll work from this very day
Until all these kids are satisfied
In the great old US of A

So all of you on Wall Street
And you ones with corporate greed
I hope that you can sleep tonight
For hunger can be cured my friend, with but a single deed

THE TWO PERCENT

You never know when death will come
Like a stranger at your door
It comes to each and every soul
Regardless how rich or poor

This one thing I truly know
You may be rich and kind
Or living homeless on the street
We leave it all behind

For that person on a lonely street
Might have love within his heart
But the rich man with his stocks and bonds
May not get a brand new start

He thinks more about his fortune
And shall until he dies
He will end up like the camel
Trying to thread the needle's eye

They will not share their riches
Nor share a single cent
They're ruthless, cruel and selfish
They're the mighty Two Percent

THIS GAME CALLED GIN

They were sittin' around the table
You could sense their awful sin
For the devil's face is in the cards
And in this game called gin

I've seen the Pros, both young and old
Lose everything they had
And end up drunkards on the street
It truly is so sad

I can see them through my window
Late at night upon the street
They all thought that they were Pros
But each one I did beat

Most of them were blowhards
They would scream and they would yell
But when the game was over
They were headin' straight towards Hell

You see the hair piece on the wall
That one with silver curls
It was the last thing that he owned
I think his name was Earl

For I'm the master tried and true
When Gin it is the game
And just so you don't forget it
Tommie is my name

SILVER STUDDED BELT

I met her in a little bar in Tulsa
Her eyes they showed the sadness that she felt
Her high heeled boots and skin tight jeans that evening
Were touched off with a silver studded belt

I slowly tipped my hat and asked her kindly
To join me over a friendly glass of beer
She slowly turned and raised up from the barstool
Her warm blue eyes were shining from the tears

She sat down at my table
Her buckle shining like the sun
And all around that sterling buckle
Were the names of all the races she had won

This barrel racing cowgirl was so lonely
And finally I asked the reason why
She said the horse I rode he was the winner
And said the things I love they always die

She said it's kinda like my folks when I was little
They bought that horse for me one summer day
Then suddenly just two short weeks thereafter
An angel came and took them both away

It was for them I rode that horse and we were winners
And he turned into the best friend that I had
This morning I found him in the meadow
Lying dead sir and that's why I am so sad

I slowly took her hand and held it gently
And told her about the sorrow in my past
But I told her that the pain that she was feeling
Would leave but all good memories they would last

And now my son we sit here at her table
And now my boy I know just how you've felt
But your Mommy's not alone she is with loved ones
She's an Angel with a Silver Studded Belt

THE WORDS WERE NEVER SPOKEN

I saw him falling to the ground
His grey uniform turned to red
He motioned for me to listen
This is what the Rebel said

"Oh yank I am a going home
For I can hear trumpets in the sky
God has picked the time and place
For this soldier boy to die"

"How I'll miss my family
And that little piece of land
Now I'm feeling so lonely
Yank, won't you hold my hand?"

A silver tear fell from his eye
Rolled down his youthful face
The musket balls had riddled
His white shirt with cotton lace

He said "If you're a wonderin'
Why I'm dressed up oh so grand
You see my wife she made this shirt for me
For luck, don't you understand?"

"Please just tell my family
How I fought so hard and brave
And that now I rest at Fredericksburg
That is where they will find my grave"

His final breath was drawn
As I held him in my arms
A year then passed and found me
On his small Virginia farm

I told his wife how brave he'd fought
In his shirt with lace so fine
The words were never spoken
That the musket balls were mine

FRIENDS FOREVER (GEORGE)

I've had friends and I've had acquaintances
And there's a difference between the two
An acquaintance will walk away
While a friend stands tried and true

He went with me on a double date
With the girl that I would wed
Would never repeat my private thoughts
Or the ramblings from my head

But then the time did drift away
Our lives found different roads
Off to the Marines and then the railroads
He shouldered a heavy load

History became his calling
Artifacts, mounds, and such
And now I've had a chance to tell him
How I missed him oh so much

Fifty years had passed us by
Then on a summer day we met
Now every day we call and chat
We aren't quite finished yet

OLD AGE

This hair that once was curly
Has turned grey and grown thin
This wrinkled face like leather hard
Hides a face that once did grin

These steel green eyes that once did flash
Have finally begun to dim
The Stetson hat I used to wear
Now lies worn with crumpled brim

My heart that once was carefree
Lies like stone within my chest
Now all I have in this worn old frame
Is to know I've done my best

For when I lost a battle
I still never ran away
But gathered strength within my soul
To fight another day

I did share my all with everyone
My family and my friends
My beliefs, my dreams and fantasies
With my all I did defend

Old age you cannot win this race
For I'm a soldier oh so brave
So as I cock my hammer hard
I will beat you to the grave

TOM'S LAST POEM

My life is almost over
This poem it is my last
My mind it now is set upon
The memories of the past

Many races during my life I ran
And I paid a heavy cost
For even though I tried my best
So many of them I lost

I've done many things I'm not proud of
At the time I could not see
I was a skilled sinner living on the edge
Even God turned his back on me

There was no fame or glory
But this poem I had to tell
I now face my life with deep regret
And wait to take my place in Hell

PART TWO
FAITH

PREACHER MAN

Just a worn and tattered bible
And a smile upon his face
A shirt that's worn and faded
That once had ruffled lace

But in his voice you can feel the magic
When he talks about the Lord
Of the fire and the brimstone
And the justice of his sword

He walks the city sidewalks
Saying children please believe
That Jesus is our savior
He can save both you and me

His church is the lonely sidewalk
And his home a city street
For he's as homeless as the homeless
But God's made his life complete

His riches are the souls he saves
And the kingdom that he shares
His diary is that tattered book
And all that's written there

He walks the city sidewalks
Saying children please believe
That Jesus is our savior
He can save both you and me

On a winter's night the preacher
Went to join his Lord above
And all of us will miss him
This man we had come to love

In his hand a tattered book
That spoke of praise and grace
And a little cross was lying
Upon his shirt of lace

Now his soul it walks the city sidewalks
Saying children please believe
That Jesus is our savior
Cause he saved a man like me

A CHRISTIAN NEVER DIES

When He comes to take me home at last
I hope my friends don't cry
For in my heart I've always known
That a Christian never dies

God has promised me His heaven
His home way up above
There will be no pain or hatred
Only His eternal love

There won't be any darkness
For His love, it shines so bright
And anywhere that you may go
You'll be walking in His light

Don't think that I have left you
I'll be with you every day
I'll be there when you slip and fall
And hear you when you pray

Then someday we will meet again
To never, ever part
So death my friends, is not the end
But is a brand new start

So when at last He takes me home
How happy I will be
And as you gather, one and all
Oh please, don't cry for me

IT HAPPENED TO A WARRIOR

It has happened to a warrior
Upon his final day
It has happened to a grieving spouse
Who fell face down to pray

It has happened to an addict
Who lay dying on the street
It has happened to the homeless
Whom we frown on when we meet

On that day that you do find Him
No more dark days full of strife
Instead you will have His kingdom
And His gift, eternal life

So regardless of your status
Owning not an earthly thing
Just remember you are royalty
And your Father is The King

So give thanks for all the dark skies
Give thanks for all the rain
Give thanks for all life's torment
The suffering and pain

For it is then that you may find Him
Within your darkest hour
To be saved by His redeeming grace
And receive His awesome power

COUNT YOUR BLESSINGS

We sang "Count your many blessings
Name them one by one"
And at that moment, I realized
That the greatest gift was God's one and only Son

I counted just a handful
Then my eyes they filled with tears
I realized that the greatest blessing
Is to know I need not fear

The greatest gift is my walk with God
He walks with me each day
He always hears my wants and needs
When I bow my head to pray

It's knowing that there is nothing
In this whole wide world to fear
My face turns to a smile
And I wipe away the tear

Just then a ray of sunshine
Broke through the stained glass pane
And I knew that my Maker
Would take me through the hardships and the rain

My second blessing is my family
Who is always oh, so dear
My third comes from the Spirit
Who says, "Because of my Son you have no fear"

Without this fear comes such a peace
Peace that floods one's very soul
And it comes straight from God
With whom you and I can accomplish any goal

ASK HIM IN

When at your lowest moment
And all your strength is gone
Look up to God and grit your teeth
Then with your faith hold on

He is life's greatest answer
To all problems big and small
He will carry you to mountains high
And catch you when you fall

With His strength he will defend you
No matter what the foe
His armor will protect you
Wherever you may go

In those times when you truly need Him
When you gaze at a sky of blue
Just ask Him in and then believe
For there is nothing he can't do

LITTLE CHURCH

A little church called Pleasant Grove
Have I loved for many years
For that's where I found my savior
Who can wipe away my tears

The people there are family
Sisters and brothers, can't you see
They even loved a sinner
I know cause it was me

The pastor taught me all I know
About heaven, earth and hell
I won't forget the sermons
And the stories he did tell

He pointed out my sinful life
And what would have been my fate
He showed me how to walk with God
And right through the pearly gate

That church it is family
Turning grey skies into blue
I'm sure that if you'll ask them
They also will love you

JOSH

I've watched your family come into church
And sit upon the pew
And the bond you have between you
Is a love so pure and true

I have watched you sit with twinkling eyes
Not missing one small thing
As the preacher talks of the Lord on high
You are a child of the King

Because of this you are a victor
A conqueror o'er this world's all
So when you walk upon your way
With faith, stand firm and tall

When you wake up on Christmas morning
And you hear the church bells ring
Don't ever forget the greatest gift
That you are a child of the King

Regardless of where your road may lead
Sometimes rough with lots of bends
There is one thing you must truly know
Josh, you can always call me Friend

A LITTLE SIGN

A little sign on the court house wall
Is displayed in this friendly town
Though truer words were never spoke
Some folks want to take it down

Just four little words, "The World Needs God"
Outlined on this sign of blue
And most folks here in the little town
Believe these words are true

But, if you are offended
By these words and what they say
Maybe when you come to this little town
You might turn the other way

But leave the sign on the court house wall
For there it does belong
With its four little words, "The World Needs God"
Its message is not wrong

CALVARY

He climbed the hill at Calvary
To die upon a cross
And took away the sting of death
Giving us victory over loss

When we think just what this means to us
Sometimes our minds can't comprehend
To walk with Him into eternity
Among our loving family and dear friends

To receive this gift it is so simple
That at times we just don't see
It's just to say in heart and mind
Lord, Savior, I do believe

Today is a new beginning
Of a walk that will last through time
Where there is no pain or suffering
Just His precious love sublime

LIFE'S RACE: MY DAD'S 85TH BIRTHDAY

The victory comes each and every day
With the setting of the sun
Then one can look to God above
And know today's race has been won

For each new day's a challenge
And it takes courage, faith and grit
But the joy comes with the conquering
And knowing you'll never quit

Thirty one thousand and twenty five
That's the number of races you have run
And with His help along the way
That's how many you have won

With all of that experience
You will win a whole lot more
For life's trophy is just seeing
What the Good Lord holds in store

EARTHLY JOY

No greater earthly joy I know
Than to serve the Lord above
To share with all, salvation
And his eternal love

The message is so simple
Sometimes we do not see
That Jesus gave eternal life
When He died for you and me

Let me spread his word forever
Wherever I may go
To tell the story of my Lord
To those who do not know

His gift it is for everyone
That's the story I will tell
And just how much he loves us
I know this oh so well

OH LORD

Oh Lord I come to you this morning
With a weak and weary heart
Hoping Lord that you'll forgive me
So we'll never ever part

Reach down and walk beside me
On this rough and rugged road
I am falling oh my Father
Underneath life's heavy load

All I'm asking oh my Father
Is you hear me when I cry
I am losing in life's battle
But you know that I did try

I've lost my job Sir and my family
Now my home it is this street
In the shadows all around me
All I see is defeat

I'm not asking for a handout
On this cold December day
Just a chance to earn a living
Can't you hear me Lord I pray

And help the others who are homeless
For this night will be so long
They say that things are getting better
Well we know that they are wrong

Give them a shelter and some food Lord
And try to keep them warm
If you don't Lord they will stumble
And won't make it through this storm

I hope you've heard me oh my Father
For the night now takes this day
And my body it is shivering
And I must be on my way

PLEASE HELP ME LORD

Lord I come to you this morning
With a weak and weary heart
Asking Lord that you'll forgive me
So we'll never ever part

Please reach down my Father
And lighten up this load
For God I am falling
On this rough and rugged road

I know I'm the one that drifted
And am the one to blame
For I surely went the distance
Before calling out your name

I suppose a man must travel
In darkness for a spell
Before he starts to realize
That his road it leads to hell

I have seen old Satan's fire
And looked him in the eye
Now God I know you're real
Please hear me when I cry

Please give me all you promise
To fight all that is wrong
And I will lift my voice to you
And praise you with a song

EDDIE K

Today I received a little book
And I don't know where to start
For the page for me to read today
Was marked with the King of Hearts

It is a book for alcoholics
And I am ONE tried and true
But if each day you read this book
It will tell you what to do

I believe the KING'S my Savior
Dwelling deep within my heart
And He along with this little book
Gives me a brand new start

If you're an alcoholic
You too can stand straight and tall
But if one day you fail
We will be there when you fall

We are a band of broken brothers
Facing each and every day
What great relief we all can find
By kneeling down to pray

I'll keep this book tucked in my vest
Until the day I die
Because it tells so much about
Our Savior in the sky

PART THREE
FAMILY

A MAN NAMED JOHN

John he was my grandpa
A coal miner was his trade
It was so very long ago
My memories sometimes fade

I remember when I was a lad
He would return from that old mine
His skin was black just like the coal
And his breath would smell like wine

He raised a family as best he could
In a mine shack dark and dim
Then I knew within my heart
I would never be like him

At night he roamed the lonely bars
To ease his life of hell
To me he was so distant
To his friends he was so swell

No harder man did ever work
So depressed and oh so blue
But I always will admire him
Cause I never walked in Grandpa's shoes

MY HERO

We all have to have a hero
To admire along life's way
I truly found the best of all
Please listen to what I say

He used to wipe my tears away
When I was a fair haired lad
And he never, ever spanked me
On those times that I was bad

He would listen to my troubles
And say, "Hey, it will be alright"
He could always smile your fears away
On a cold and wintry night

Then I grew into a teenager
And every day was spring
I didn't need my hero much
For I knew most everything

Then I grew into a young man
And looked the world square in the eye
God how I did stumble
Regardless how hard I tried

At times when all seemed hopeless
I could call him on the phone
And just to hear my hero's voice
I would not feel alone

Now I'm in my golden years
And I am oh so glad
For my hero's never let me down
You see, he is my Dad

THE HARDEST POEM I EVER WROTE

This poem is for my Father
And the words are hard to rhyme
For it speaks about a friend of mine
And the love that will last through time

I will never forget old Sanford and Son
As we fished and sipped a beer
But when my mind brings back those times
My eyes they fill with tears

You truly are my very best friend
And we have had a heck of a ride
And never ever did I feel alone
With you there by my side

I would confide with you about everything
Including the birds and bees and such
I would tell you of that special girl
The one I loved so much

There never was a moment
When you ever let me down
And I never saw that smile of yours
Turn with disappointment into a frown

We both are getting older
Getting ready for a brand new start
I will end my rhyme by saying
"I love you with all my heart"

DAD

Today's our father's birthday
This man of ninety years
The memories do flood our hearts
And our eyes fill with tears

We remember summer vacations
Rocky Mountains capped with snow
Clear blue lakes in Minnesota
Where wild rice does grow

He taught us how to bait a hook
So the big fish we would snare
And by listening to him carefully
We found it okay to swear

"That little bastard got away
As I was trying to set the hook"
Then when he knew we heard him
He would give that guilty look

The five of us did travel
From shore to shining shore
And the love we shared together
Who could ask for any more

And we gather now to thank you
For all of the times we've had
But more than that we want to say
We truly love you, Dad

I'LL ALWAYS LOVE YOU

You're the only one I ever loved
And love I can't explain
My heart was always yours alone
Please forgive me for the pain

For you I would have died
Still would unto this day
I hope you do forgive me
That's what I ask for when I pray

I was young and foolish
And never meant you harm
But my love belonged to only you
Waiting on a Midwest farm

You were my little sidekick
The one that had no fear
I never grew into a man
To wipe away your tears

I just ask you for your patience
For I will make it up to you
But one thing, Love, do not forget
My love for you is true

GIRL ON A PEDESTAL

Your first love is so special
No words can err explain
The way she loves so tenderly
To wipe away life's pain

The laughter, tears and summer nights
Makes a man's eyes turn to tears
For the starlit nights of long ago
Are just memories of yester year

My life I can't live over
And the ride it was not fun
But the girl upon the pedestal
Will be there till my race is run

LOVE OF MY LIFE

There are no words that can express
The love I feel for you
A lover, friend and confidant
My very best buddy too

We have had a ride so thrilling
For nearly fifty years
You have shared my joys and dark times
There to wipe away my tears

I would like to give you diamonds
Or a rainbow in the sky
But instead I give my very soul
Until the day I die

LOVE

I will love you oh my darling
Throughout ages, throughout time
Now I will tell you just how much
In a story that does rhyme

This love's more precious than all the gold
That lies buried in the hills
It's pure as white spring waters
Not made up of fleeting frills

It's a pain that lies within my chest
At times when you're away
And the joy that I do feel
When you walk into my day

I would trade all of life's fortunes
My ego and my pride
To have you for a moment
To be there by my side

I give thanks to the Mighty Master
Who sent you down from up above
For giving me this greatest gift
An Angel whom I do love

A PIECE OF WOOD

No one will know the guilt we shared
As the poem went on the wood
But we knew down deep within our souls
That we were doing all we could

God sent so many Angels
After that Christmas morn
Your mom and I received our love
And a heavenly Love was born

Angels came forth as humans,
As we stood there on the brink
With gifts of faith of encouragement
Though we had lost the kitchen sink

Now, our precious little daughter
Here is what '82 it did for you
It taught you independence
And to yourself be true

In '82 we wanted
To give you all we could
But all we had was a family's love
And a poem on a piece of wood

CIRCUIT PREACHER

If you would have lived in the wild, wild, west
A long, long time ago
You would have been a circuit preacher
That's one thing I do know

I can picture you in a buggy with frills
With a Bible by your side
With not a fear as you roll along
Because with Jesus you did abide

We think about wild outlaws
And law men, all so tall
But the humble circuit preacher
Had more courage than them all

Sometimes you spoke to strangers
Whose eyes pierced you like a sword
And you had the courage to ask them
"Do you really know our Lord?"

But you are living in the present
A circuit preacher of modern day
And we hope with all our heart and soul
That on this course you'll stay

ANDY VISITS GREAT GRANDPA

He tells me stories of days gone by
Of things of long ago
Of how he met my Great Grandma
His sweetheart don't you know

He tells me of his childhood days
When there weren't a lot of toys
And how he played so many games
With other little boys

Great Grandpa is so much fun
For he holds me on his lap
A lot of ways he's just like me
He too takes lots of naps

He's also kind of just like me
For we both walk kind of slow
Sometimes we come unto a place
And forget which way to go

Sometimes when he tells me stories
We'll by lying on the floor
But before the story's over
Great Gramps begins to snore

When Daddy comes to get me
I'll never know just why
But when Great Grandpa tells me goodbye
The tears they fill his eyes

A BIRTHDAY GIFT FOR ANDY

Andy is the birthday boy
And is 2 years old today
But Grandpa didn't buy you toys
That would someday go away

My present, Andy, is outside
So take me by the hand
And I'll give to you the finest gift
That there is upon this land

The first gift is a dandelion
As yellow as the sun
And when it dries you can blow on it
And have all kinds of fun

The second gift's a robin
With her nest up in this tree
Very soon she'll have her little ones
For Andy and me to see

The third gift is this sea of red
Fresh strawberries on the vine
Let's sit right down and eat a few
That one's yours and this one's mine

The fourth gift is that rainbow
Stretching across the sky of blue
I have told you about the pot of gold
And Andy, I think it's true

The fifth and final gift I have
Is the greatest one of all
For it will be there always
Even when you're big and tall

This final gift is a thing called love
That all Grandpa's have for their little boys
And will always be more precious
Than all their games and toys

A STAR IS BORN

I want to tell you all a story
About a boy who rose to fame
This young lad's name was Andy
And baseball was his game

He was playing in the outfield
Upon that fateful day
His team was behind 17 to 1
And we all began to pray

Then the pitching coach he pointed
To Andy and the mound
And there upon that sunny day
A true pitcher, friend, was found

This little pitcher, four-foot-three
Looked the batter in the eye
And the wind up, then the smoker
Left the batter with just a sigh

Three batters up and all went down
To this mighty little man
With heart and determination
And the will that says "I can"

From that day a star was born
Now he's in the Hall of Fame
This little boy named Andy
With baseball as his game

ANDY

The other night I could not sleep
As many old men they'll do
Then I thought of our Grandson Andy
And how proud we are of you

It's not about the diploma
Or when your hat flies in the air
But the dedication that you've put forth
And the effort that got you here

And there's one thing I truly know
And hope to see before I die
That whatever it is you choose in life
It's with the Eagles you will fly

It is not about the winning
Or where a man must start
It's about life's race that you must run
And the secrets in your heart!

ANDY: A FINE YOUNG MAN

The time has passed so quickly
Changing a child into a man
We watched as you began to crawl
And finally to stand

Then baseball games and summer fun
White clouds and skies of blue
Your life – a kaleidoscope
And we enjoyed the view

And very soon this fine young man
He will be college bound
Now, more than just a Grandchild
Our best friend we have found

Wherever life's road does lead you
If we are near or far apart
The best advice we give to you
"Always listen to your heart"

LEWIS AND EVELYN

Sixty years of being as one
And how the time does fly
Lives filled up with memories
That money cannot buy

Our joy would be this thing called love
That we have shared throughout the years
For it was with us in our laughter
And also wiped away some tears

Our gift would be five daughters
And with them our love we shared
And only God will ever know
How much we truly cared

Our world now is the Grandkids
Sharing stories, songs and rhymes
And relating adventures of long ago
In a golden time

Now our treasurers are the little things
A smile, a glance, a touch
For all of them mean just one thing
That I love you oh so much

ME AND BARBARA JEAN

My sister and I had a special place
It was our Grandpa's piece of land
Not really large 'nuff to be a farm
Just a strip mine, coal and sand

In springtime Grandpa would hitch the horse
To a single bottom plow
And I would ride her all day long
Looking back I don't know how

Barbara Jean and I, we loved the west
And dreamed of mountains high
We vowed someday to buy a ranch
But sometimes dreams do die

Grandpa's house sat on a hillside
And up the hill sat a barn
And we would straddle that wooden gate
And for hours trade cowboy yarns

There were so many good times
Our Uncle Bob he took a wife
And we learned in life that there are sad times
When Uncle Don he took his life

I have never broke a promise
And I promise you Barbara Jean
That dreams they always do come true
We will see that ranch with grass so green

ABOUT THE AUTHOR

Tom Paulding was born and raised in Iowa. He and his wife, Mary Frances, currently live in Hillsboro, Illinois. They have a daughter, Ramona, and a grandson, Andy.